A. W. West

A short history of Ohio

A centennial souvenir

A. W. West

A short history of Ohio
A centennial souvenir

ISBN/EAN: 9783743334892

Manufactured in Europe, USA, Canada, Australia, Japa

Cover: Foto ©ninafisch / pixelio.de

Manufactured and distributed by brebook publishing software
(www.brebook.com)

A. W. West

A short history of Ohio

A SHORT

HISTORY OF OHIO.

By A. W. WEST,
Principal High School, ~~Miamisburg~~, Ohio.

AND

J. L. HUNT,
Principal Grammar School, Germantown, Ohio.

A Brief Sketch of the Leading Events in the History of Ohio, and an Outline of its Civil Government. Many Valuable Facts and Statistics are Appended.

A CENTENNIAL SOUVENIR.

DAYTON, OHIO:
PRESS OF UNITED BRETHREN PUBLISHING HOUSE.
1888.

A Short History of Ohio.

Antiquities.

There are more than ten thousand ancient earth-works found within the territorial limits of Ohio. They are of great antiquity. The Indians had no tradition of their origin. These remains are usually divided by archæologists into three general classes; namely, *mounds*, *effigies*, and *inclosures*. A good example of the *mound* is situated on the bank of the Great Miami River, near Miamisburg. It is symmetrical in form, and has a height of sixty-eight feet. In this class of mounds are usually found one or more skeletons. Such mounds were constructed, not only as places of burial and sacrifice, but as places of observation.

Perhaps the most notable *effigy* within the State is situated near Brush Creek, in Adams County. It represents a serpent, more than a thousand feet long, in the act of swallowing, or ejecting, an oval figure. Such mounds are supposed to have been the special objects of adoration and worship of their builders.

The best example of *inclosure* within the State is Fort Ancient, in Warren County. It is situated on a plain, two hundred and thirty feet above the Little Miami River. Its embankments are nearly four miles in length, and inclose one hundred acres. This class of works was, doubtless, constructed in most cases, as places of defense.

3

Mound Builders.

The prehistoric people who constructed these mounds, we call *Mound Builders*. We have neither written record nor tradition of their origin or destiny. The only means by which we may arrive at a knowledge of these people, is the study of their numerous and remarkable remains. That the Mound Builders were a people of common habits, customs, religion and government, is proven by the number, great extent and uniformity of their works.

Ohio Indians.

The Indian tribes of Ohio possessed the character common to the North American Indian. Very little was known of the Ohio Indians before the year A. D. 1750. At this time, some knowledge of them had been obtained from Indian traders, and from explorers. The principal Indian tribes occupying the Ohio territory at that time, were the Wyandots or Hurons, Delawares, Shawanese, Miamis, Mingoes, Ottawas and Chippewas. The *Wyandots* occupied principally the region of the Sandusky River; the *Delawares*, the valleys of the Tuscarawas and Muskingum Rivers; the *Shawanese*, the valleys of the Scioto and Mad Rivers; the *Miamis*, the valleys of the Great and Little Miami Rivers, and the *Mingoes* occupied places on the Ohio River, also, on the Scioto River. The *Ottawas* were confined to the region of the Maumee and Sandusky Rivers, and the *Chippewas* lived on the southern shore of Lake Erie.

French Exploration and Settlement of the Northwest Territory.

The Northwest Territory was the name given to that great stretch of country lying northwest of the Ohio River, now constituting the States of Ohio, Indiana, Illinois, Michigan and Wisconsin, and that part of Minnesota east of the Mississippi. French missionaries and explorers were first to penetrate this region, on the southern shores of the Great Lakes, in the early part of the seventeenth century. Their object was the conversion of the Indian to Christianity, and the extension of the empire of France by exploration and settlement. Leaving the French posts in Canada, Marquette and Joliet discovered the Upper Mississippi in 1673. La Salle discovered the Ohio River in 1669. Reaching it from one of its upper tributaries, he and his companions dropped down the river to the "Falls" at Louisville. In April, 1682, La Salle reached the Mississippi River from the outlet of Lake Ontario, after making the third attempt. He sailed to its mouth, giving to the world the first written account of the "Father of Waters." France claimed the entire Mississippi Valley by right of discovery and settlement, and continued to exercise this right for more than a hundred years. La Salle tried to secure this vast domain to France, by erecting a chain of forts from the mouth of the Mississippi to Canada. Before England had taken steps to secure the Mississippi Valley by settlement, flourishing French settlements had been established at Detroit, Peoria, Kaskaskia, Vincennes and New Orleans; besides some forty or fifty forts had been erected in various parts of the country. La Salle named the country watered by the Mississippi and its tributaries, Louisiana, in honor of his "Grand Monarch," Louis XIV.

English Right of Possession.

England claimed possession, not only of the Northwest Territory, but of all territory lying west of the coast line explored by the Cabots, in 1497 and 1498. This right was reaffirmed in all her grants to the colonies, as these grants extended from "ocean to ocean." Besides possessing this title of discovery, the English had acquired large portions of the Ohio Valley by treaty with the Iroquois or Six Nations.

The First Ohio Land Company.

The first "Ohio Land Company" was organized in Virginia, in 1748, by some of the Washingtons and Lees, together with some London merchants, for the purpose of establishing settlements west of the Alleghanies. They received a grant of half a million acres, to be located principally on the south side of the Ohio River, between the Kanawha and Monongahela. In 1750, this company sent out Christopher Gist to survey their land, and to make explorations in the Ohio Territory. Gist was the first white man of Anglo-Saxon descent to visit in an official capacity the country now comprised within the limits of Ohio. Crossing the Ohio River at or near the present site of Pittsburgh, he continued his journey westward to the Tuscarawas River, which he descended to its junction with the Walhonding. From this point he continued his course westward, crossing the Scioto, and finally reaching the English trading post, Pickawillany, established in 1749, on the Great Miami River, at the mouth of Loramie's Creek. Gist made his way to the Ohio River, which he descended to the "Falls." He returned through Kentucky to his home in Virginia.

Pickawillany.

Pickawillany is called "the first point of English settlement in Ohio." It was built in 1749. George Croghan and Andrew Montour made liberal presents to the Miamis in behalf of Pennsylvania, who, in return, gave them permission to erect a trading-house at the mouth of Loramie's Creek, in the present county of Shelby, for the benefit of Indian trad-

6

ers frequenting this region. This stockade was of brief duration, for in 1752, the French, assisted by the Chippewas and Ottawas, attacked the traders and their Indian allies, killing fourteen of the garrison, chiefly Miamis, and carrying off many prisoners to Canada.

Other Events Preceding the French and Indian War.

Indian Treaty.

In 1744, certain lands on the Ohio had been obtained by purchase of the Iroquois, at a council held at Lancaster, Pennsylvania. This treaty being held in distrust by the Western Indians, Virginia sent three commissioners to treat with the Indians at Logstown, a small trading post situated on the north side of the Ohio, seventeen miles below Pittsburgh. In June, 1752, a full confirmation of the Lancaster treaty was obtained, and also permission to construct a fort at the forks of the Ohio.

Movements of the French.

The French were active in maintaining possession of the Ohio Valley. Plates of lead, bearing French inscriptions, were buried at the mouths of the principal tributaries of the Ohio in the summer of 1749. English traders were expelled from the country, and the Governor of Pennsylvania was warned to encroach no further on French territory. The French had established themselves in considerable numbers at Presque Isle, Le Boeuf and Venango, in readiness to repel any encroachment of the English.

Washington's Journey.

Desiring to avert hostilities, Governor Dinwiddie, of Virginia, sent Major George Washington, then a young man of twenty-two, on an important diplomatic mission to the French commandant at Fort Le Boeuf. The message demanded reparation for losses inflicted on English traders, and declared the rights of the colonists to the disputed territory. With three attendants, Washington left Williamsburg, October 31st, 1753, and after a journey of over four hundred miles, reached the French Post of Venango, December 4th. Learning the intentions of the French at this place, he resumed his journey to Fort Le Boeuf, the headquarters of Saint Pierre, the chief commander. Receiving a written answer to Dinwiddie's remonstrance, he retraced his journey, exposed to hostile Indians and the snows of winter, and after the lapse of eleven weeks he again stood in the presence of the Governor. Washington noted carefully the extensive preparations of the French for military operations. These preparations confirmed the answer of Saint Pierre, declaring his intentions to possess the Ohio Valley.

Fort Duquesne.

In March, 1754, the Ohio Company sent Captain Trent, with a party of thirty-three men, to build a fort on the site of Pittsburgh. While they were building this fortification, Captain Contrecoeur, with one thousand Frenchmen, in sixty bateaux and three hundred canoes, floated down the Alleghany and took possession of this fort, naming it Fort Duquesne.

French and Indian War.

The capture of the English fort, at the source of the Ohio, was immediately followed by a nine years' conflict, between the French and English, known as the "French and Indian War." This war decided that the vast central valley should bear for all coming time the impress of the English, instead of the French civilization. By the Peace of Paris, signed February 18th, 1763, France ceded to England all claim to the Ohio Valley. Other territorial changes were also made.

Pontiac's War.

At the close of the French and Indian War, the English colonists pressed eagerly into the Ohio Valley. New settlements were planned by the Ohio Land Company. Instead of withdrawing from the territory, the French lingered among the Indian tribes, keeping alive the hatred of these tribes for the English. Pontiac, an Ottawa chief, conceiving the plan of exterminating all the frontiersmen west of the Alleghanies at one stroke, united the tribes from Canada to the Carolinas into one vast confederacy for this purpose. The success of the formation of this confederacy, the harmony of its action, and the all but successful execution of its designs, marks Pontiac as one of the greatest Indian warriors. The English occupied forts at Michilimackinac, Detroit, Presque Isle, Le Boeuf, Venango, on the Maumee and on the Wabash, at Sandusky, Fort Pitt, Niagara, and other stations inferior to these. In the spring of 1763, these posts were secretly invested with fierce savages. No warning had been given. The frontiersmen had been betrayed by tokens of peace and friendship. Suddenly, along the entire frontier, the posts and settlements of the English were attacked. Over two hundred pioneers were murdered, and nine forts fell into the hands of the savages. Extermination of the frontiersmen was narrowly averted. Detroit was closely besieged for eight months. Michilimackinac was taken by stratagem, and half of its garrison murdered. Fort Miami was taken by the same artful means. Presque Isle, Fort Le Boeuf and Venango fell into the hands of the savages. Fort

9

Pitt was besieged for several months, until relieved by an expedition led by Colonel Bouquet. The relief of Fort Pitt, and the failure to capture Detroit and Niagara disheartened the Indians. Knowing that their attempt to exterminate the whites would be followed by severe retaliation, the tribes quickly withdrew from the confederacy. The original feuds prevailed. Pontiac was deserted by all, save a few faithful followers. Pontiac went to the tribes in Illinois. After living among them several years, he met his death at the hands of an Indian while endeavoring to form a new conspiracy against the whites.

Moravian Missions.

Early Missions.

In 1761, Rev. Christian Post and James Heckewelder were first to attempt the founding of a Moravian mission among the Delaware Indians of the Muskingum Valley. Ten years later, Rev. David Zeisberger founded a Moravian station called Schönbrun, situated on the Muskingum, two or three miles from the present town of New Philadelphia. In the same year, a second mission was established a few miles below the former, called Gnadenhütten. From time to time other missions were formed among the Indian tribes of Eastern Ohio. They were centers, where pious men taught the "children of the forest" the rules of civilized life.

Perils of the Moravians.

At the time of the Revolution, the situation of the Moravian missions was rendered very unfavorable to the growth of these peaceable communities. Situated midway between the hostile Wyandots and the frontier settlements of Western Pennsylvania and Virginia, also between the British posts in the Northwest and the American military post at the

"Forks of the Ohio," now Pittsburgh, they were subjected to many wrongs from these hostile parties. They were charged by the Indian tribes with friendship for the pioneers, and by the pioneers with complicity with Indian incursions on the frontier settlements; by the colonists with sympathy for the English, and by the English with being spies for the colonists. The crisis soon came.

Removal to Sandusky.

In 1781, Captain Elliott, a British emissary, forced the removal of these Christian Indians to the banks of the Sandusky. There they made a settlement called "Captive's Town." After a winter of great hardship, about one hundred and fifty of their number were permitted to return to their former homes to gather corn for the subsistence of the mission.

Massacre of Moravians.

In March, 1782, a force of about ninety men under command of Captain David Williamson, was collected together at Mingo Bottom, three miles below the present city of Steubenville, for the purpose of punishing the Indians for atrocities then recently perpetrated on the whites. They resolved to hold the "Christian Indians" responsible for these outrages. Marching to their former homes on the Upper Muskingum, there they found parties of these exiles, who had returned, gathering corn in their own fields. Disarming more than ninety of these Indians and imprisoning them in two well guarded houses, the work of death began. But two of this number escaped. This massacre has been characterized as "the most disgraceful event in the history of the country."

Subsequent Missions.

After the massacre of the Moravians, in March, 1782, n mission existed in the Ohio territory until 1786, when Rev James Heckewelder and others established a mission on th Cuyahoga River. It was mainly composed of the remnan of those who had lived on the Muskingum. Missions cor tinued to exist within the present limits of the State in more or less precarious condition until 1824, when by th retrocession of their lands, in the Tuscarawas valley, to th general Government, the Moravian missions among the Ohi Indians ceased to exist.

The distinguished Moravian missionaries, Heckewelde and Zeisberger are regarded as among *the founders of Ohi* so eminent were they and so long were they connected wit its history.

Bradstreet's Expedition.

In the summer of 1764, Colonel Bradstreet, with an arm of nearly twelve hundred men, sailed up Lake Erie to the re lief of Detroit, then besieged by Pontiac. After relievin this post, he sent a detachment to take possession of Mack nac. Treaties were concluded with the Indians, by whic their lands became a part of the royal domain.

Bouquet's Expedition.

While Colonel Bradstreet was relieving Detroit, Colon Bouquet was preparing to invade the country of the Ohi Indians from Pennsylvania. He organized an army at Ca lisle, consisting of six hundred English regulars and Vi ginians. Leaving Fort Pitt, he had almost reached the Ir dian villages on the Muskingum, when he was met by abor fifty chiefs and warriors of the Delawares, Shawanese an Senecas, who sued for peace. Colonel Bouquet demande return of all prisoners, which they promised to make. After another conference in October, the Indians promised a return of captives in twelve days. At the forks of the Muskingum, on the day appointed, was witnessed the surrender of over two hundred captives. Another pledge was given, and hostages taken for its fulfillment, that all other prisoners held by these tribes, such as could not be brought in on so short notice, would be surrendered the next spring. In the following May, about one hundred additional prisoners were surrendered at Fort Pitt. A treaty of peace was concluded, after which the Ohio frontier was comparatively free from Indian warfare for about ten years.

McDonald's Expedition.

In the spring of 1774, some Indian atrocities were perpetrated on the frontier settlements. War soon resulted from the mutual hatred existing between the Indian and the encroaching pioneer. The kindred of Logan, the Mingo Chief, had been murdered under circumstances of great perfidy by a party of about thirty men, commanded by Daniel Greathouse. War could not be averted. Lord Dunmore authorized Colonel Angus McDonald to recruit a force west of the Alleghanies for the purpose of moving against the Indians. The combined force, after joining with that of Captain Michael Cresap, numbered four hundred. They penetrated the Indian country to a point midway between the present towns of Zanesville and Coshocton. This expedition resulted in a few skirmishes with the Indians, and the burning of some of their towns. Nothing substantial was accomplished.

Lord Dunmore's War.

Desiring to make a campaign against the Indians, Governor

13

Dunmore organized an army of fifteen hundred men, principally from the northern counties of Virginia. Colonel Andrew Lewis enlisted some twelve hundred men in the southern counties. These two armies were to form a junction at the mouth of the Great Kanawha. Bancroft says, "These armies were composed of noble Virginians, who braved danger at the call of a royal governor, and poured out their blood to win victory for western civilization." Crossing the Ohio River near Marietta, Governor Dunmore dispatched a messenger to Colonel Lewis, then encamped at the mouth of the Kanawha, commanding him to join the main army near the Indian towns on the Scioto,

Battle of Point Pleasant.

Early on the morning of the 10th of October, 1774, when the division of Colonel Lewis was making preparations to march, they were suddenly attacked by a thousand Shawanese, led by the chiefs, Cornstalk and Logan. This battle continued all day. The Indians were repulsed, but the Virginians lost in killed about seventy-five, and in wounded about twice that number. The next day after the battle, Colonel Lewis went in rapid pursuit of the Indians in the direction of their villages on the Scioto.

Treaty at "Camp Charlotte."

A treaty was concluded at "Camp Charlotte," with the principal chiefs on the Scioto. The Indians, who had just returned from their defeat at the battle of Point Pleasant, were eager for peace. After the conclusion of the treaty, Governor Dunmore withdrew his forces, greatly to the displeasure of Colonel Lewis, who was anxious to prosecute the war. For the purpose of protecting the frontier settlements,

14

small forces were left at the mouth of the Kanawha, at Fort Henry (now Wheeling), and at the "Forks of the Ohio."

Logan's Speech.

Logan, the Mingo Chief, would not appear in the council at "Camp Charlotte." He alone refused to recognize peace. Dunmore, being anxious to obtain his recognition of the treaty, sent Colonel John Gibson to "Chilicothe town," across the Scioto, where Logan usually staid when not on the "war-path." It was on the occasion of this interview that Logan expressed himself in those eloquent and pathetic words which have made his name famous. Logan's kindred had been murdered, and as he thought by a party of whites led by Michael Cresap. It has been proven that Michael Cresap, a gallant soldier and a pure patriot, was in no way connected with this outrage. Speaking to Colonel Gibson, Logan says: "I appeal to any white man to say if he ever entered Logan's cabin hungry, and he gave him no meat; if he ever came cold and naked, and he clothed him not. During the course of the last long and bloody war, Logan remained idle in his cabin, an advocate for peace. Such was my love for the whites, that my countrymen pointed as they passed, and said, 'Logan is the friend of the white man.' I even thought to have lived with you, but for the injuries of one man. Colonel Cresap, the last spring, in cold blood and unprovoked, murdered all the relations of Logan, not even sparing my women and children. This called on me for revenge. I have sought it. I have killed many. I have fully glutted my vengeance. For my country, I fully rejoice at the beams of peace. But do not harbor the thought that mine is the joy of fear. Logan never felt fear. He will not turn on his heel to save his life. Who is there to mourn for Logan? Not one!"

British Allies.

Six months previous to the treaty at Camp Charlotte, occurred the battle of Lexington. British emissaries were early dispatched to the tribes of the northwest to enlist their aid in the royal cause. Congress attempted the establishment of treaty relations with these tribes. They sustained a doubtful neutrality with both contending parties during the year of 1776. But English influence prevailed, and the Indian tribes of the Northwest became allies of the British. Congress sought to avoid war with the Indians in this crisis. Encroachment on Indian territory was forbidden. It was not until 1778 that an expedition was planned against these Indians and Detroit, the stronghold of the British in the northwest.

General McIntosh's Expedition.

(1778.) General McIntosh, in command of about one thousand men, left Fort Pitt with the object of marching against Detroit, and the Indian towns on the Sandusky. Reaching the Tuscarawas, he erected a stockade, which he called *Fort Laurens*, at the present town of Bolivar, in Tuscarawas County. This was the first substantial stockade erected on Ohio territory. Colonel Gibson and about one hundred and fifty men were left to defend this post. The expedition returned to Fort Pitt. The garrison was not properly supported, and harassed by the Indians, they were compelled to abandon Fort Laurens in 1779.

Colonel Bowman's Expedition.

(1779.) To retaliate for atrocities then recently committed in Kentucky by Ohio Indians, Colonel John Bowman, with one hundred and sixty men, marched against the Shawanese villages, on the Little Miami River, within the present limits

16

of Greene County. Crossing the Ohio near the present city of Cincinnati, they reached the strongest of these villages at the end of the second day's march. The troops were divided into two divisions, one of which was commanded by Colonel Benjamin Logan. They attempted a surprised attack, but, "from some unexpected cause, there was no efficient co-operation between the two wings of the Kentucky army, and consequently but little success." One Indian village was destroyed and a portion of the growing crops. Nine of Colonel Bowman's men were killed. The chief, Blackfish, was wounded. The Kentuckians made a hasty retreat to their homes beyond the Ohio. This expedition emboldened the Indians to further depredations on the whites.

Colonel Clark's Expedition.

In July and August, 1780, Colonel George Rogers Clark, in command of about one thousand Kentuckians, crossed the Ohio at the mouth of the Licking and marched against the Indians on the Little Miami. Arriving at "Old Chillicothe," on the banks of the Little Miami, they found this village had been burned in anticipation of their approach. Proceeding to Piqua, an Indian town on Mad River, they were attacked by a party of Indians in ambush. Twenty Kentuckians were killed. The Indians were repulsed; their town and crops destroyed. The expedition returned to Kentucky, where it was disbanded. During the preceding winter Colonel Clark made an expedition* against the British

---

* Judge Chase says in his sketch of Ohio: This expedition was attended with important consequences. It annihilated the British authority on the Mississippi, detached several Indian tribes from the British interest, inspired the rest with a salutary dread of American arms, and had important influence on the negotiations which afterward established the Mississippi as the western boundary of the United States.

posts in Illinois. Despite great hardships, this bold Virginian, with a force of less than two hundred men, captured Vincennes and Kaskaskia, and added this vast dominion to Virginia. It was then erected into the County of Illinois.

Colonel Crawford's Expedition.

(1782.) After the massacre of the Moravians, (March 8, 1762,) a new expedition was formed, under command of Colonel William Crawford. Leaving their encampment on the Ohio, near the present city of Steubenville, this expedition, with a force of nearly four hundred men, marched to a point on the Sandusky, three miles north of Upper Sandusky, where a battle was fought June 4-5. Colonel Crawford was defeated with a loss of more than one hundred men in killed and prisoners. On the third day of the retreat, Colonel Crawford was captured by a party of Delawares. He was carried to Tymochte Creek, a few miles west of Sandusky, where he was put to death under circumstances of the greatest cruelty.

Colonel Clark's Expedition.

In 1782, a second expedition was made by Colonel George Rogers Clark against the Indians of the Miami Valley. The disastrous battle of "Blue Licks" had caused a spirit of retaliation among the pioneers of Kentucky. A number of Indian towns on the Great Miami were destroyed, and also Loramie's store, in the present county of Shelby.

Titles to Ohio.

The territory lying northwest of the Ohio River, and drained by it, was, doubtless, in a remote age, in the exclusive possession of the Mound Builders. We may conclude, from the number and extent of their works, that they devel-

18

oped to the dignity of a nation, and exercised control of this vast domain. When discovered by the Europeans, it was in the peculiar possession of those Indian tribes already enumerated. (See Ohio Indians.) From the time of the voyages of La Salle to the treaty of Paris, in 1763, France exercised authority over this territory, though in defiance of titles set up by Great Britain. The Ohio Valley remained in the possession of Great Britain until the treaty of peace was concluded at Paris in 1783, when it passed under the control of the United States. In 1784, by the treaty of Fort Stanwix, the title of the Six Nations to the Ohio Valley was extinguished. When the Revolution closed, New York, Massachusetts and Connecticut asserted claims to portions of the territory now included within the limits of Ohio, and Virginia asserted claims to all of it. These titles were based upon grants from the English sovereign. New York made a deed of cession to the United States in 1782; Massachusetts, in 1785; Connecticut, in 1786, retaining the Western Reserve, which was finally ceded in 1801. In 1784, Virginia through her representatives, Thomas Jefferson, Samuel Hardy, Arthur Lee and James Monroe, ceded all her territory lying northwest of the Ohio River (except the Virginia Military District), to the general Government.

The "Ordinance for Freedom."

An ordinance for the government of the newly acquired "Northwest Territory," was passed by Congress, July 13, 1787. Nathan Dane, of Massachusetts, was chairman of the committee that reported, July 11th, "An Ordinance for the Government of the Territory of the United States Northwest of the Ohio." It discarded the unjust law of primogeniture, which had existed in the colonies. It also provided that "there shall be neither slavery nor involuntary servitude in said territory, otherwise than in the punishment of crime, whereof the party shall have been fully convicted." Rev. Manasseh Cutler, more than any other man, secured the passage of the clause prohibiting slavery. The ordinance was a fundamental law for the government of the "Northwest Territory," with which all its subsequent laws, both Territorial and State, were made to conform.

Organization of the Ohio Company.

In March, 1786, General Rufus Putnam and General Benjamin Tupper called a meeting at Boston, of Revolutionary officers, for the purpose of organizing a company to purchase and settle lands west of the Alleghanies. The company was formed with General Rufus Putnam, General Samuel A. Parsons, Rev. Manasseh Cutler and General James N. Varnum as directors. Rev. Manasseh Cutler and Major Winthrop Sargent, agents of the company, made application to the Board of the Treasury for the purchase of lands. This purchase was perfected, October 26, 1787, and embraced about a million and a half of acres, situated within the present counties of Washington, Athens, Meigs and Gallia, subject to reservation for educational, religious and charitable purposes. Bancroft says of this company: "It interested every one. For vague hope of colonization here stood a hardy band of pioneers, ready to lead the way to the rapid absorption of the domestic debt of the United States; selected from the choicest regiments of the army, capable of self-defense; the protectors of all who should follow them; men skilled in the labor of the field, and artisans, enterprising and laborious, trained in the severe morality and strict orthodoxy of the New England villages of the day."

Settlement at Marietta.

Immediately after the purchase of lands on the Muskingum by the Ohio Company, they began the organization of a colony for its settlement. At a meeting of the directors, held November, 1787, General Putnam was chosen president of the company. In December, 1787, a number of mechanics and boat-builders assembled at Danvers, Massachusetts, and departed for the head waters of the Ohio. A month later they arrived at Simrall's Ferry on the Youghiogheny. In January, General Rufus Putnam and party, consisting of proprietors and surveyors, left Hartford, Connecticut, for the same point. The two parties met at Simrall's Ferry, where they built a boat of fifty tons burden, which they called the "Mayflower." "Her bows were raking, or curved, like a galley, and strongly timbered; her sides were made bullet-proof, and she was covered with a deck roof." By April 2d, they had constructed a sufficient number of boats to transport the colony to its new home. In the afternoon of the same day, the fleet, consisting of the "Mayflower," one flatboat and three canoes, dropped down the river. They reached Kerr's Island, about three miles above the present site of Marietta, on the morning of the fifth day following, and about noon of the same day, they landed on the east bank of the Muskingum, about four hundred yards above its mouth. When General Putnam landed at the mouth of the Muskingum River with forty-eight colonists, April 7, 1788, the germ was planted which in one hundred years has developed into the great civilization of the "Northwest."

Laws for the Government of the Colony.

"The emigrants under command of General Rufus Putnam, landed their boats at the upper point of the Muskingum River, Marietta, on the 7th of April, 1788, where they unloaded their effects. The boards which they brought with them for the erection of temporary huts were landed and properly disposed of. A large tent was put up for the governor of the colony, General Putnam and in this tent he transacted all the business of the colony. On the 9th of April, 1788, the Governor's chart of laws was read by his private secretary, General Benjamin Tupper, and approved by the members of the colony association:—

"'First.—Be it ordained by the Officery and Council, that said territory be one district, subject to be divided into five districts, as future circumstances may make it expedient.

"'Second.—Be it ordained that the Governor and Officery may make such laws, civil, criminal and military, for the Colony, but not to conflict with the laws of the original re-established United States laws of 1787.

"'Third.—Be it ordained that the Grand Council be composed of three Supreme Judges and three Territorial Association Judges, before whom shall be tried and decided all the business of the Colony, civil, criminal and military.

"'Fourth.—The Grand Council will hold their sessions, 5th July; 8th, 9th of April, and 2d Wednesday, September, annually, where all claims against the association must be presented and canceled.

"'Fifth.—Be it ordained that the Governor receive at the rate of forty dollars per month for his services while performing the duties of his office. All other Officery and Grand Council, one dollar per day while in the performance of their duties, martial, military, musicians, chaplain, singers and teachers of schools.

"'Sixth.—Be it ordained that all permanent emigrants to the Territory, shall be entitled to one hundred acres of land free, within the Nortwest purchase.

"'Seventh.—Be it ordained that all pioneers and their descendants may become life and benefit members of the Emigrant Association, Northwest Territory, by paying $1 per annum to the Governor, for the use of the association.

"'Eighth.—Be it ordained that all members must entertain emigrants, visit the sick, clothe the naked, feed the hungry, attend funerals, cabin raisings, log rollings, huskings; have their latch-strings always out.

"'Ninth.—Be it ordained that all members of the Colony, from the ages of eighteen to forty-five, must perform four days of military duty per annum. All uniformed companies may drill once a month, dates and places fixed by their officers. Officer drills once a year.

"'Tenth.—Be it ordained that all members of the Colony must celebrate the 22d of February, 7th of April, and 4th of July annually. Also in proper manner observe the 28th of November, 25th of December, and 1st day of January annually.

"'Eleventh.—Be it ordained that every member must keep the Sabbath by attending some place of religious worship agreeably to the dictates of his own conscience.

"'Twelfth.—Be it ordained that common schools should be established as soon as emigration to the Territory is sufficient.

"'Thirteenth.—Be it ordained that a library of historical and school books be established at the Governor's headquarters, and that General McIntosh, who is now engaged in writing a history of the colony, will serve as legal agent for that purpose; also, Colonel Timothy Flint act as an assistant. Also, that all official appointments be made by the Governor of the Colony and confirmed by the Grand Council. Be it further ordained that the Metropolis be named

Marietta, in honor of Queen Marie Antoinette, of France, who gave aid and influence during the darkest days of the Revolution. Ordered that three copies of this territorial chart of ordinances be copied and posted, as ordained: One at Fort Harmar, one at the East Point, and one at the Stockade. These ordinances to take effect on the 1st day of May, 1788 (Queen Marie's birthday).

"'By the Governor of the Northwest Territory, 9th of April, 1788.

"'RUFUS PUTNAM.

"'By his Private Secretary, N. W. T.,

"'BENJAMIN TUPPER.'"

Civil Government Established.

Governor St. Clair arrived at Marietta, July 9, 1788, and six days thereafter he, with Judges James N. Varnum, Samuel H. Parsons, and Secretary Winthrop Sargent, formally established civil government in the Northwest Territory. Judge John Cleves Symmes had not yet arrived. On the 25th, a law was published for the organization of the militia; and two days thereafter, all the territory east of the Scioto, or nearly one half of the present State of Ohio, was erected, by proclamation of the Governor, into the County of Washington. On the 2d of the following September, the first Court of Common Pleas in the territory was opened at Marietta with imposing ceremonies. Rufus Putnam and Benjamin Tupper were judges of the court; Return Jonathan Meigs, clerk, and Ebenezer Sproat, sheriff. Paul Fearing, the first lawyer in the Territory, was admitted to practice on the day the court was organized.

Growth of the Colony.

Before the close of 1788, eighty-four new colonists had

joined the original number. The new city was laid out with great regularity. It included the interesting remains of an ancient fortified town. On one of the reverses was built an extensive block-house, called "Campus Martius." "This fortification, designed to be one of the strongest in the West, was laid out in a perfect square, surmounted by a watch-tower at each angle." It was strongly fortified at the beginning of the Indian War, in 1791. Several houses were erected and clearings made. In the winter of 1788-89, there was a scarcity of provisions. Flour could not be had, and boiled corn or coarse meal was substituted for it. The deer and bears, upon which the colonists wholly relied for animal food, had been well nigh exterminated by the Indians. In January, a great flood occurred in the Ohio, from which all settlements along this river suffered. Before the close of the year 1790, two settlements had been begun at Belpré, a fertile tract of land at the mouth of the Little Hockhocking; and two others at Waterford and Millersborough, twenty miles above Marietta, on the Muskingum. At the latter place, the first mill in Ohio was in successful operation.

Education in the Colony.

The "Ordinances of 1787" contained the following famous article: "Religion, morality, and knowledge being necessary to good government and the happiness of mankind, schools and the means of education shall forever be encouraged."

The founders of the colony at Marietta, were men of education, and in many instances men of mark in the nation 's history. Early attention was given in the colony to education of the youth and to public worship. The directors of the colony were requested to employ, if possible, "an instructor eminent for literary accomplishments and the virtue

25

of his character." Schools were opened as rapidly as the population of the colony would permit. General Rufus Putnam was especially active in the cause of education. He was the leading spirit in the organization of the first educational institution west of the Alleghanies. The building of the Muskingum Academy was proposed in 1797, and was opened as an institute of learning in 1800. David Putnam, a graduate of Yale College, was first teacher.

Rufus Putnam.

Rufus Putnam, founder of Ohio, was born at Sutton, Massachusetts, April 9, 1738. He was left fatherless at the age of seven years. His early life was beset with very great disadvantages, yet by self-denial and great industry he obtained a fair English education. At the age of fifteen he became the apprentice of a mill-wright at Brookfield. Four years later he enlisted as a private in the French and Indian War. He made an expedition to Florida in 1773, and two years later entered the Continental Army as a lieutenant-colonel of a regiment at Roxbury. As an engineer he played a memorable part in the siege of Boston. Before the close of the Revolution, he was commissioned as brigadier-general. For a time after the Revolution he was land agent and surveyor for his native state. Being one of the chief promoters in the organization of the Ohio Company, he was chosen the superintendent of the company, and managed its affairs until the arrival of Governor St. Clair at Marietta, July 9, 1788. He presided over the first court held in the Northwest Territory. He was appointed by Washington as Surveyor-General of the United States. Rufus Putnam was one of the trustees of the university at Marietta from the date of its origin till the close of his life. He died in Marietta, Ohio, May 1, 1824.

Symmes' Purchase.

Soon after the purchase of the "Ohio Company," John Cleves Symmes, of New Jersey, made a similar purchase of one million acres, fronting on the Ohio and lying between the Great and Little Miami Rivers. The purchase was subsequently so modified, by act of Congress, that it only amounted to 311,682 acres, exclusive of reservations.

Columbia.

While Judge Symmes was attempting a settlement at South Bend, Major Stites, of Pennsylvania, made a settlement at the mouth of the Little Miami River, called Columbia. He landed here with a party of twenty-six men about the middle of October, 1788, and constructed a block-house. This was the first English settlement in the Miami Valley, and the second in Ohio.

Founding of Cincinnati.

Settlement was begun where Cincinnati now stands, December 28, 1788, by Mathias Denman and others. They soon completed a survey for the town, which was called *Losantiville*. In 1790, Major Doughty built Fort Washington here. In January, 1790, Governor St. Clair arrived at the post and organized the county of Hamilton, which was made to include all the territory lying between the Great and Little Miami Rivers. Cincinnati was made the county-seat. Governor St. Clair officially abolished the name "Losantiville," and named the town *Cincinnati*, in honor of a society of soldiers which was known by that name.

Harmar's Campaign.

Two treaties were concluded with the principal Western tribes at Fort Harmar, January, 1789. After prolonged deliberation, the Indians consented to terms of peace. But it soon became evident that the savages had but little regard for these treaties. During the summer and autumn of 1790, Indian depredations on the frontier settlements were frequent. Parties floating down the Ohio from the settlements about Marietta were often attacked and murdered by the Indians. Governor St. Clair, having learned that the Northwest tribes were preparing for war on the whites, determined to send an expedition against these Indians. This expedition, consisting of about fourteen hundred troops, left Port Washington under command of General Harmar, September 30, 1790. After a toilsome journey of seventeen days, they encamped among the Indian villages on the Maumee. After a few days' inaction, a detachment was sent out under Colonel Hardin, which was ambushed and suffered a severe repulse. Having destroyed the deserted villages, General Harmar ordered a homeward march. Colonel Hardin with a force of three hundred and sixty returned to the Indian villages to renew the attack. He was again defeated by an overwhelming number of Indians concealed in the tall grass. Colonel Hardin lost more than half of his men. Major Willis, who led the regulars, fell. The army retired to Fort Washington.

Effect of Harmar's Campaign.

Instead of checking the Indian depredations, the disastrous defeat of Hardin and the destruction of their villages only incited the savages to a more vigorous prosecution of the war. During the winter of 1790-91, no frontier settlement was free from attack. The pioneers in the exposed settlements found safety in the military stations at Marietta, Belpré, and Waterford. Spies or rangers were employed to traverse the forest and to keep close watch of the foe. These were men whose courage, endurance and knowledge of Indian warfare especially fitted them for such a duty.

St. Clair's Expedition.

To hold back the barbarians from sweeping down on the exposed settlements along the Ohio River, Congress prepared to construct a chain of forts from the head-waters of the Maumee to Fort Washington. General St. Clair was intrusted with this undertaking. Leaving Fort Washington September 6, 1791, with an army of two thousand men, he advanced twenty miles northward, where Fort Hamilton, on the east bank of the Great Miami, was constructed and garrisoned. Advancing forty-two miles farther, they constructed Fort Jefferson. Leaving this post, the army encamped on one of the tributaries of the Wabash, in what is now the southwest angle of Mercer County, at nightfall, November 3d. The foe hovered about the encampment. St. Clair resolved to construct some defenses the following morning and await the arrival of a detachment, sent to the rear, to escort their train of provisions. They were attacked, however, in the early morning (November 4th) by Little Turtle with more than two hundred warriors. St. Clair was defeated with great loss. His army had been weakened by the desertion of three hundred militia and the absence of one regiment of regulars. Pressed upon all sides by the savages, it was with great difficulty that his shattered columns drove the enemy from the possession of the road, and escaped destruction. Major Butler, second in command, was killed. The survivers retreated to• Fort Jefferson. St. Clair lost more than eight hundred in killed and wounded. This defeat subjected General St. Clair to

29

unlimited abuse. He was tried by a military tribunal and pronounced free from blame. General Anthony Wayne was appointed his successor.

"In December, 1793, detachment was sent forward by General Wayne to build a fort on the site of St. Clair's defeat. It arrived there on Christmas day. The ground, now free from snow, was covered with remains of the dead. The next day pits were opened and the bones were reverently buried. Six hundred skulls were found upon the field. After this melancholy duty had been performed, a fortification was built, which was called *Fort Recovery*."

Wayne's Expedition.

After St. Clair's defeat, no less than five attempts were made to settle the difficulties with the Indians by treaty. They failed. Knowing that these failures to obtain peace would be followed by hostilities on the part of the Indians, General Anthony Wayne, with an army of three thousand men, broke up camp at Cincinnati and marched to Greenville, where he spent the winter of 1793-94. The next summer he took up his march to the Maumee, and there built Fort Defiance, at its junction with the Auglaize. After building Fort Adams on the St. Marys, he made an encampment near the British post called Fort Miami, which is situated at the foot of the Maumee Rapids. With an ample force to defeat the savages and lay waste their country, but wishing to avoid bloodshed, General Wayne made proposals of peace. They were rejected. Breaking up his camp he advanced to the head of the rapids, near the present site of Maumee City, where he attacked and signally defeated the Indian tribes of the Northwest, August 20, 1784, in what is known as the "Battle of Fallen Timbers."

fter some sharp correspondence with the English com-
andant at Fort Miami, because of his occupation of ac-
1owledged territory of the United States, General Wayne
1ally retired into winter quarters at Greenville.

Treaty at Greenville.

The Indian war, which had scarcely subsided since 1791,
as concluded with the Treaty at Greenville, negotiated
1gust 3, 1795. Eleven hundred and thirty Indians par-
:ipated in this treaty. It established peace, and defined
e extent of the lands of these tribes. The boundary line,
en recognized, followed the Cuyahoga River and the Tus-
rawas to Fort Laurens, thence due west to Fort Recovery,
ence southerly, striking the Ohio near the mouth of the
entucky.

Rapid Settlement.

After the conclusion of the Treaty at Greenville, the settle-
ents in the Ohio Territory had no more to fear from Indian
rays. The pioneers emerged from the block house to
1ild new homes unharmed. The population of the North-
est Territory began to increase rapidly. New settlements
ere made about Marietta, and numbers of Revolutionary
:terans of Virginia found homes in the Virginia military
servation. The valleys of the Miamis became the scene
rapid and prosperous settlement. Citizens from Conne&-
ut were beginning settlement in the Western Reserve.
egular mail service was established between Cincinnati
1d Pittsburg, July, 1786. In the same year the British
acuated the northwestern posts.

Second Grade of Territorial Government.

In 1798, the Northwest Territory contained "five thousand
2e male inhabitants of full age," the requisite number to

entitle it to an elective legislative assembly, as provided by the "Ordinance." The General Assembly consisted of governor, legislative council, and house of representatives. The first election in the Territory was held on the third Monday of December, 1798. Members of the legislature were chosen. This body nominated ten men, from which body the president chose five to act as legislative council. Members of the council were elected for a term of five years, and representatives for a term of two years each. The governor had unlimited veto power. The first meeting of the General Assembly for the Territory convened at Cincinnati, September 16, 1799. Thirty bills passed at the first session, but Governor St. Clair vetoed eleven of them. It is thought that the free exercise of the veto power by the governor of the Northwest Territory was the cause of the very limited prerogatives subsequently granted to the governors of Ohio under the State Constitution. William Henry Harrison was chosen delegate to Congress. On May 7, 1800, the seat of government was changed to Chillicothe, and on the same day Congress created Indiana Territory, which was made to include the present States of Indiana and Illinois. The third session of the legislature adjourned, January 23, 1802, to meet at Cincinnati in November following, but that fourth session was never held. The Ohio Territory was found to contain a population sufficient to permit its admission into the Federal Union.

Admission of Ohio.

There has been much discussion concerning the exact date of Ohio's admission to the Union, The facts are as follows : On April 30, 1802, Congress passed and enabling act, authorizing the people of the territory to frame a State constiution. The constitution was framed by a convention that met on the 1st, and adjourned on the 29th of November, 1802. Some consider this last as the date of admission, and the great seal of the State bears the date—1802; but the territorial government continued until Congress passed an act recognizing the State of Ohio, which received President Jefferson's signature on February 19th, 1803. By this act Ohio was admitted. It provided for the "due execution of the laws of the United States within the State of Ohio." The act declares "that the said State shall be one district, and be called the Ohio district; and a district court shall be held therein, to consist of one judge," etc. On March 1st, 1803, the first General Assembly met at Chillicothe, and the State government went into operation. Edward Tiffin became Governor on March 3d, 1803.

The Settlers.

Homes.—The first settlers lived in log cabins. To construct these, they had what were called "house-raisings." The neighbors entered heartily into this work, and as whiskey was cheap in those days, it was used freely at these and similar gatherings. A large open fire-place was constructed in one end of the cabin, and used for both heating and cooking. Wooden pins supplied the place of nails. Boards for floors, shelves, tables, etc., were hewn out of logs with the ax. Door hinges and latches were made of wood, and "the latch string always hung out." Windows were made of oiled paper.

Food.—Every man was a hunter, and the flesh of deer, wild turkey, squirrel, and bear furnished a large portion of his food. The squirrels were so thick that the children had to chase them away from the corn fields. At a later day pork took the place of the flesh of wild animals. Corn-bread was the staff of life, and as mills were scarce, it generally took the settler several days to take his "grinding" to mill and return. Mush and milk served for the evening meal. "Johnny-cakes" were frequently baked on a board. A frying-pan, kettle, and "Dutch" oven were the cooking utensils of fifty years ago. Stoves and matches had not been introduced.

Clothing.—Nearly all of the clothing worn was of home manufacture. Flax was spun, and woven into linen for towels and summer clothing. Wool was carded and spun, and woven into cloth, for clothing. In almost every house could be found a spinning-wheel and loom. Deer skins were much used by men for outer garments. Common cotton check was $1 a yard, and five yards were deemed an ample dress pattern. Lucky was the girl who could get such a bridal dress.

Furniture.—Almost every article, such as split-bottomed chairs and stools, was made at home. A ladder or pegs in the wall led to the loft, where the younger members of the family generally slept. The buckeye tree was a friend to the pioneer. From its fibers, hats were made, and from its trunk were carved the tray for the delicious "pone" and "Johnny-cake," the venison trencher, the noggin, the spoon, and the huge white bowl for mush and milk.

Frolics.—Dancing and social parties were called "frolics." Corn-huskings, barn-raisings, log rollings, and weddings were always followed by frolics. There were many "fiddlers," and dancing was much in vogue.

When first settled, Ohio was almost entirely covered with forest. Before corn, potatoes, tobacco, pumpkins, etc., could be planted, a "clearing" must be made. The trees that

34

could not be cut down and removed, were "deadened." The "clearings" were added to year by year. At the present time less than one fourth of Ohio is covered with forest. In early days it was necessary for the farmer to haul his produce to the nearest river port, and exchange it for such things as he needed. Commercial prosperity came only with the introduction of canals and railroads.

Early Towns. 1911992

Gallipolis was laid out in 1791, by French settlers.
Manchester was laid out in 1791, by Nathaniel Massie.
Hamilton was laid out in 1794, by Israel Ludlow.
Chillicothe was laid out in 1796, by Nathaniel Massie.
Steubenville was laid out in 1798.
Springfield was laid out in 1801, by James Demint.
Newark was laid out in 1802.
Dayton was laid out in 1795. It was named after Jonathan Dayton, the leader of the settlers. Nineteen settlers arrived, April 1, 1796.

The Government employed Ebenezer Zane to cut out a road, or "trace," through Ohio, from Wheeling to Maysville, Kentucky. "Zane's trace" was opened in 1797. He was given three sections for his road-making, and took one where his road crossed the Muskingum, another where it crossed the Hocking, and the third where it crossed the Scioto. He laid out on these tracts, Zanesville in 1799, and Lancaster in 1800, and would have owned the site of Chillicothe, had not the bank of the Scioto River been within the Virginia military reservation.

"Whisky was a cheap and popular beverage in the so-called 'good old days,' and it exercised a most harmful influence over several of the young settlements. Chillicothe

35

nearly succumbed to it at one time, Zanesville was a heavy sufferer for years, and Lancaster experienced similar difficulties.

"Shortly after Lancaster was laid out, and while the stumps still remained in the streets, a few of the settlers persisted in drinking heavily, and winding up each night with a frolic or fight. There was no law at that time available, and the better elements determined to take the matter into their own hands.

"A meeting was called, and it was decided that any person who was found intoxicated, should for every such offense be compelled to dig a stump out of the street, or suffer personal chastisement. The result was happy. No one ever cared to dig up a stump again after having had the experience; so, for a time, drinking ceased, and law and order reigned. But this question of intemperance and its solution has proved a pretty 'hard row of stumps,' and it would be a relief if resort could be had to the simple methods of the early settlers."

Cleveland, the "Forest City," was laid out in 1796, and was named after General Moses Cleveland, who had charge of Government surveys in the neighborhood.

Fort Industry was built on the present site of Toledo, in 1800. Here an Indian treaty was made, July 4, 1805.

Mormons.—In 1832, the Mormons, under the leadership of Joseph Smith, settled at Kirtland, Lake County. They started a bank without a charter, and many people were swindled out of their money. The society declined in numbers and respectability, and in 1838 removed to Missouri.

Land Grants.

After the Revolution, all of the States surrendered their claims to what is now Ohio, to the general Government, except Connecticut and Virginia. The principal land tracts and grants are as follows:

1. Ohio Company's purchase, 1,500,000 acres along the Muskingum.

2. Symmes' purchase, between the Little Miami and the Big Miami Rivers.

3. Western Reserve; Connecticut reserved about 4,000,000 acres of land in Northeastern Ohio. Of this, 500,000 acres, known as "Fire Lands," were donated to sufferers by fire in the Revolution. The remainder was sold for $1,200,000, which became the foundation of her school fund.

4. Virginia Military Land between the Scioto and the Little Miami Rivers, reserved for bounties to Revolutionary soldiers.

5. The United States Military Reservation in the central part of the State.

6. Congress Lands, sold by the Government to the settlers.

7. Canal Lands, College Lands, the French Grant, and a few others, were small tracts.

8. School lands. One thirty-sixth part of all lands were set apart for educational purposes.

From time to time, treaties were made with the Indians, by which they gave up all claims to Ohio lands.

Blennerhassett.

Herman Blennerhassett, a wealthy and gifted Irishman, built a princely mansion on a beautiful island in the Ohio, near Marietta. This "second paradise" was the general resort for all the country round. His beautiful and accomplished wife reigned the queen of this kingdom of taste and refinement. Into this house Burr came, and induced its owner to become his chief associate in the scheme to found a southern empire. The lovely island was made the chief resort of the conspirators, and many Ohio people aided them; but they quickly deserted them when ten boat loads of their supplies were captured on the Muskingum, and four more were seized at Marietta by Government troops. (1806.) Blennerhassett escaped from the island, but was afterwards captured. He was soon released, however, and it is believed that he saw no treasonable design in Burr's expedition. The soldiers sacked the elegant mansion. They became drunk, and committed outrages which would have disgraced any band of savages. One of the drunken wretches fired a bullet through the ceiling of the large hall, the ball passing through the chamber near where Mrs. Blennerhassett was sitting with her children. The shrubbery, flowers, and orchards were ruined. Thus the loveliest spot, perhaps, on the continent, was transformed into a scene of desolation and ruin. Soon after, the dilapidated mansion, with its furniture, fine library, and expensive philosophical apparatus, was destroyed. After years of wandering, Blennerhassett died in poverty on the Island of Guernsey. Mrs. Blennerhassett returned to this country, and was petitioning Congress for remuneration for the loss of her early home, when she died, in 1842.

Ohio in the War of 1812.

Hull's Surrender.—General William Hull, Governor of Michigan Territory, started from Dayton, Ohio, with twelve hundred Ohio volunteers and three hundred regulars for the purpose of invading Canada. After advancing into Canada to no purpose, he retreated to Detroit. When the enemy came up, he ordered the white flag (a table-cloth) to be displayed, although his men were anxious to fight and confident of victory. (August 16, 1812.) He not only surrendered Detroit, but the whole of Michigan Territory. He was tried by court-martial, and being convicted of cowardice, was sentenced to be shot. The President pardoned him on account of his Revolutionary services.

Fort Meigs.—In the beginning of 1813, General Harrison was made commander of the Army of the West, which was concentrating at the head of Lake Erie. General Winchester had been stationed at Fort Defiance on the Maumee. General Harrison now erected Fort Meigs on the Maumee Rapids, near old Fort Miami. Here he was attacked by Proctor and Tecumseh. General Clay, with twelve hundred Kentuckians, having come to the rescue, the British and Indians gave up the siege, after treating their captives with the usual barbarities.

Fort Stevenson.—1813. Proctor besieged Fort Stevenson, at Lower Sandusky (now Fremont), garrisoned by only one hundred and fifty men under Major Croghan, a brave young soldier, only twenty-one years of age. Proctor called on the garrison to surrender in order to escape massacre. The heroic Croghan answered, that, when the fort was taken, a massacre would do no harm, for none of its defenders would be left alive. Croghan had but one cannon. By firing it from different places he tried to make the enemy believe that he was well provided with artillery. The British concluded to take the fort by storm. Croghan concealed his cannon so as to sweep the ditch through which they had to pass. When the ditch was full of men, he opened fire with deadly effect. The British now retreated after a loss of one hundred and fifty men, while the Americans had but one killed and seven wounded. Croghan was promoted to the rank of colonel, and the ladies of Chillicothe gave him an an elegant sword.

Perry's Victory.—Oliver H. Perry built, with many difficulties, a flotilla, consisting of the Lawrence, Niagara, and seven smaller vessels, at Erie, Pennsylvania. He then proceeded to Put-in-Bay. Near this place, on September 10th, 1813, Perry, with his fleet of fifty-four guns, defeated Commodore Barcley with a fleet of sixty-three guns. Perry sent this memorable dispatch to General Harrison: "We have met the enemy, and they are ours; two ships, two brigs, one schooner, and one sloop." It was the first time in the naval history of Great Britain that an entire squadron had surrendered. A marble monument was erected, in memory of Perry's heroic services, at Cleveland, 1868. A large picture in the capitol at Columbus represents Perry standing erect in the face of a hot fire from the enemy, while he is being rowed, in a small boat, from the Lawrence to the Niagara.

Harrison crossed into Canada and defeated the British at the battle of the Thames. Tecumseh was killed and Proctor fled.

Capitals.—The State capital has been located at the following places:

Chillicothe,	1800—1810.
Zanesville,	1810—1812.
Chillicothe,	1812—1816.
Columbus,	1816 to the present.

In 1796, Lucas Sullivant, a young Virginia surveyor, laid out the town of Franklinton on the west bank of the Scioto River, opposite the present site of Columbus. It had a population of 3,000 in 1812.

Columbus is one of the three towns in the United States born a capital. In 1812, Lyne Starling, John Kerr, Alexander McLaughlin, and William Johnson secured the establishment of the seat of the State government on the high bank (then covered with forest), east of the Scioto River, opposite Franklinton. They gave to the State a ten-acre square

40

for public buildings, and built thereon a state house, penitentiary, and other buildings, costing·$50,000, When the legislature held its first session in the modest brick state house, in 1816, the rude hamlet contained a population of seven hundred souls. This old capitol building was destroyed by fire in 1855. Governor Morrow laid the corner stone of the present capitol, July 4, 1839. It was completed in 1855. Columbus now has a population of 79,000, and contains among its many public buildings the largest insane asylum in the world, being one mile and a quarter in circumference.

Boundary Lines.

When Ohio was organized into a Territory in 1800, the western boundary was a "line beginning on the Ohio, opposite the mouth of the Kentucky River; thence running to Fort Recovery; thence north until it intersects the territorial line between the United States and Canada."

There was much trouble about the northern boundary line. The enabling act under which Ohio was admitted into the Union bounded the proposed State on the north "by an east and west line drawn through the southern extremity of Lake Michigan," and extending easterly "until it shall intersect Lake Erie." The ordinance of 1787 represented Lake Michigan far north of its real position, and its size and location had not been ascertained as late as 1812. It was found that the proposed line would pass from five to eight miles south of Lake Erie. Ohio maintained that it was the manifest intention of Congress to make the southern shore of Lake Erie her northern boundary, while Michigan claimed jurisdiction over the lake shore to the Pennsylvania line. Several lines were afterwards surveyed, none of which suited both States. In 1833, a party beginning a "permanent" survey was attacked by Michigan settlers, who sent them away badly beaten. In the same year the governors of both States occupied the disputed territory with small armies. Federal commissioners arrived about this time, and induced the belligerent governors to retire with their men and await the action of Congress. In 1836, Congress decided in favor of Ohio, but gave Michigan what is now her Upper Peninsula. Ohio got what she was contending for—the excellent harbor on the Maumee, where Toledo now stands.

Civil Government of Ohio.

[Compiled from State Documents.]

The present constitution of the State is a revision of the constitution of 1802, that was ratified by the people, June 17, 1851. A new constitution was rejected at the election of 1874.

Elections.—The State and county officers are elected on the first Tuesday after the first Monday in November.

Voters—All males, twenty-one years old, native or naturalized, may vote, provided they have resided one year in the State, thirty days in the county, and twenty days in the township or ward, before the day of election.

Township Government.

1. POWERS OF A TOWNSHIP.—

A township is "a body politic, and corporate, for the purpose of enjoying and exercising the rights and privileges conferred upon it by law; it shall be capable of suing and being sued, pleading and being impleaded, and of receiving and holding real estate by devise or deed; or personal property for the benefit of the township for any useful purpose."

42

. TIME OF THE ELECTION OF OFFICERS.—

The first Monday of April.

. THE TOWNSHIP OFFICERS ARE:—

(*a.*) The Township Trustees, who may divide the township into road districts, provide plows and scrapers for working the roads of said districts, may purchase gravel for such roads, may prevent the spread of contagious disease, may establish a pound for cattle, may submit the question of founding a public library and have the care of the same, may purchase hearse and vault for the township, may relieve the poor, must settle disputes as to partition fences, open roads that have been viewed favorably, etc. The road district has its own supervisor.

(*b.*) The Township Treasurer, who pays out township money on order of the clerk, and is treasurer of the board of education.

(*c.*) The Township Clerk, who must keep an accurate record of the proceedings of the trustees at their meetings, publish an account of the receipts and expenditures of the trustees and board of education, act as clerk of the board of education, record chattel mortgages, etc.

(*d.*) Constable, his duty being to serve writs and legal proceedings specified by law, make arrests, summon witnesses and jurors.

(*e.*) Assessor, whose duty it is to list and value property in his precinct, and gather certain statistics.

School property and church property are not taxable.

(*f.*) Board of Education, consisting of the township clerk and the clerks of local boards. Its duties are to levy tax for schools, apportion school funds, build, enlarge, and repair school-houses, adopt a course of study and text-books, employ a superintendent of schools, janitors, etc.

43

Each sub-district has its own local board, whose principal duty is to employ a teacher.

(*g.*) Justices of the Peace, elected every three years and commissioned by the Governor of the State, exercise jurisdiction over most of the offenses arising within their respective townships. Some of their powers are to administer oaths, solemnize marriages, acknowledge deeds, mortgages, and other written instruments, to subpœna witnesses, and compel attendance in cases coming before them, etc.

County Government.

COUNTY OFFICERS ARE:—

1. County Auditor, elected every three years. He is secretary of the board of commissioners, certifies all money except taxes into the county treasury, issues warrants on the treasury, keeps an account with the treasurer of receipts and expenditures of the county, transfers lots and land when sold, furnishes blank books to assessors, prepares a tax list, keeps an account with each school district, and apportions and distributes school funds, etc.

2. County Treasurer, elected every two years. He receives taxes twice a year, and gives receipts for the same, collects delinquent taxes, pays taxes due the State into the State treasury, must submit to semi-annual examination of his books, must publish at given times a statement of money in the treasury, may advance money collected as tax due school boards and city and village treasurers, etc.

3. County Recorder, elected every three years. His duties are to record deeds, mortgages, plats, leases, powers of attorneys to sell land, to note on such instruments the time of receipt and record, to keep an alphabetical list of instruments recorded, etc.

4. County Surveyor, elected every three years. He must make a survey of any lands in the county on application of interested parties or by order of the courts.

5. Sheriff, elected every two years. He "shall preserve the public peace, and cause all persons guilty of any breach hereof, within his knowledge or view, to enter into recognizance with sureties, for keeping the peace, and appearing at the succeeding term of the Common Pleas of the proper county; and to commit to jail in case of refusal; * * * and shall execute all warrants, writs, and other processes to him directed by the proper and lawful authority; and shall attend upon all courts of Common Pleas, and the District Court, during their sessions, and the Probate Court when required; and he shall have power to call to his aid, in the execution of the duties herein, and by law required, such person or persons, or power of the county, as may be necessary; and, under the direction and control of the county commissioners, he shall have charge of the court-house," etc.

6. Coroner, elected every two years. He must hold an inquest over the body of any person dead by violence or accident.

7. Infirmary Directors, elected for a term of three years. They have the care of the county poor.

8. County Commissioners, elected for a term of three years. They must hold four regular sessions annually, must provide a place for holding courts, shall build and repair bridges and approaches thereto, may cause water-courses to be straightened, may purchase site for and erect a court-house, and borrow money by issuing bonds for the same or for other county indebtedness, may examine the county treasurer's books, may provide orphans' asylums and children's homes, may act as school board in certain cases, etc.

45

9. Clerk of the Court of Common Pleas, elected for three years. He must keep a complete record of each case tried, unless ordered to the contrary; must report certain criminal statistics to the Secretary of State, must furnish poll books and tally-sheets for elections, must draw, in the presence of the sheriff, the names of the grand and petit jurors, etc.

10. Prosecuting Attorney, elected for two years. He prosecutes, in the name of the State, all complaints, suits, and controversies to which the State is a party, collects costs for the State, and its claims against others; is the legal adviser of county officers and boards of education, reports legal statistics to the Attorney General, etc.

11. Probate Judge, a judicial officer, elected for three years. He takes the proof of wills, admits copies of them to record, directs and controls the settlement of the accounts of executors and administrators, appoints and removes guardians, grants marriage licenses, licenses ministers to solemnize marriages, makes inquests respecting lunatic, insane, idiotic, and deaf and dumb persons, etc.

12. Judge of the Court of Common Pleas, elected for five years, presides over the Court of Common Pleas in the county or counties for which he is elected.

"The Court of Common Pleas shall have original jurisdiction in all civil cases where the sum or matter in dispute exceeds the exclusive original jurisdiction of justices of the peace; and appellate jurisdiction from the decision of county commissioners, justices of the peace, and other inferior courts in the proper county, in all civil cases, subject to the relations provided by law. It shall have original jurisdiction of all crimes and offenses, except in cases of minor offenses, the exclusive jurisdiction of which is vested in justices of the peace, or that may be invested in courts inferior to the Common Pleas."

State Government.

THE OFFICERS OF THE STATE ARE :—

1. The Governor, elected for two years; salary, $8,000. He is the supreme executive power of the State; may require information in writing of the executive officers of the State, shall communicate a message to the General Assembly at every session, may convene it on extraordinary occasions, is commander-in-chief of the military and naval forces of the State, fills vacancies in State offices, commissions all judges elected under the constitution and laws of the State, justices of the peace, and notaries; may grant reprieves, commutations and pardons, except for treason, and in cases of impeachment; may surrender fugitives from justice on demand, may appoint staff officers, commissioner of deeds, of railroads and telegraphs, statistics of labor, of fisheries, superintendent of insurance, inspector of mines, State librarian, supervisor of public printing, trustees of benevolent institutions; must be present at the count of presidential votes, issue writs for election of Congressmen or members of the General Assembly, may commission or discharge militia officers, call out the militia, etc.

2. Lieutenant-Governor, elected for two years. He is *ex-officio* president of the senate, and succeeds the Governor in case of disability, death, or removal.

3. Secretary of State, elected for two years. He has charge of and keeps safely all laws and resolutions heretofore passed and that shall be passed, countersigns and registers commissions issued by the Governor, prepares rules for county surveyors, publishes the statistics of Ohio, is State sealer, and has charge of the standard weights and measures, publishes the times of holding courts, records articles of incorporation, etc.

4. Auditor of State, elected for two years. He is the chief accounting officer of the State; money is drawn from the treasury on his warrant or legal claims, if there is money in the treasury appropriated for the same; he prepares forms and instructions for county auditors, apportions State school funds, causes forfeited lands to be sold, etc.

5. State Treasurer, elected for two years. He is entrusted with the safe keeping of State funds, and with the paying out of the same on the warrant of the State Auditor.

6. Attorney-General, elected for two years. He is to appear for the State in State cases, civil and criminal, in the Supreme Court; is to appear in any court or tribunal in any State case when required by the Governor or General Assembly; is the legal adviser of State officers and the authorities of State institutions, of the Legislature, prosecuting attorneys, etc.

7. Commissioner of Common Schools, elected for three years. He must visit teachers' institutes, confer with boards of education and school officers, counsel teachers, visit schools, lecture on educational topics, may require reports from boards of education and auditors, and prepares forms for the same ; distributes school laws, investigates complaints of the fraudulent use of school money, appoints a board of State examiners, etc.

8. Members of the Board of Public Works, elected for a term of three years. They have charge of the canals and their appurtenances, regulate tolls on the same, collect fines, rents, etc.

9. Judges of the Supreme Court, elected for a term of five years. They must meet annually on the Tuesday after the first Monday of January ; may appoint a law librarian and a reporter. The original jurisdiction of the Supreme

Court extends only to quo warranto, mandamus, habeas cor_ pus, procedendo. Its appellate jurisdiction extends to judgments and decrees of courts created and organized in pursuance of the provisions of the constitution.

10. Clerk of the Supreme Court, elected for three years. He "shall prepare all needed dockets, and attend all the sessions of the courts, and enter and record all orders, judgments and decrees, and proceedings of the Supreme Court and the Supreme Court Commission, and issue all needful writs and processes."

11. Circuit Court. The State is divided into seven circuits. The Circuit Court consists of three judges in each circuit, elected for three years. Two terms are required to be held in each county each year. This court has like original jurisdiction with the Supreme Court. It has also jurisdiction in error from the Common Pleas Court to reverse, vacate or modify a judgment or final order of said court, in actions triable therein by jury, and jurisdiction by appeal from said court in cases tried therein in which the right to demand a jury did not exist. Salaries of judges, $4,000 per year.

12. General Assembly. The General Assembly convenes annually on the first Monday of January. It consists of thirty-six Senators and one hundred and eight Representatives, elected for two years. A bill becomes a law after receiving the votes of a majority of both branches. Salary of members, $600 a year and twelve cents mileage.

13. United States Circuit Court. The State is divided into two United States districts, a northern and a southern. Each district is divided into an eastern and western division. This court is held in Cleveland, Toledo, Columbus and Cincinnati.

Canals.

Ohio has seven hundred and ninety-six miles of artificial water-ways, including six hundred and fifty-eight miles of canals proper. The first canal was commenced in 1825, and the last one completed in 1842. The total cost was $14,688,-666, being an average of $18,453 per mile. The Ohio Canal, from Cleveland to Portsmouth, with feeders, is three hundred miles long. The Miami and Erie Canal, from Cincinnati to Toledo, with feeders, is two hundred and ninety-three miles long. St. Mary's reservoir in Mercer County, a feeder of the Miami Canal, is said to be the largest artificial lake in the world. It is about ten miles long, and from two to four miles in width. When it was completed, over one hundred and fifty residents, thinking that it would "tempt miasma," made a breach in the embankment. The grand jury failed to find a bill against the perpetrators.

These canals are still much used in carrying heavy and bulky articles, such as coal, iron, corn, wheat, lumber, and ice.

Railroads.—The Mad River and Lake Erie Railroad was chartered in 1832, and actively begun in 1835. It extended from Dayton to Sandusky, and was completed in 1848.

Three lines extended across the State in 1852. In 1841, there were thirty-six miles of railroad; in 1886, 9,200 miles.

Libraries.—By laws passed in 1853, and in 1860, books were provided for common school libraries. In 1865, there were 350,000 volumes in these libraries, but the books became scattered and lost by negligence. By a law passed in 1867, the remaining books were turned over to town library associations. At present all cities and many towns have large public libraries and reading rooms which are main-

ained by a small tax. There are now two hundred and fifty-
wo libraries in the State, containing about one million volumes.

Ohio in the Civil War.

Ohio sent 517,133 soldiers into the Rebellion, of which 239,-
76 were three year troops. Ohio saved West Virginia to the
Jnion at the very beginning. Most of the great generals were
rom Ohio. Among them are: Grant, Rosecrans, Sherman,
Sheridan, McPherson, Gilmore, Cox, McDowell, Buell, O. M.
Mitchel, Schenck, Garfield, Steedman, Crook, Keifer, and
Hayes. Stanton, Lincoln's War Secretary, was born at Steu-
enville. Salmon P. Chase was Secretary of the Treasury,
nd "the father of our National Bank system." Ben Wade
nd John Sherman were at the head of the most prominent
war committees. President Andrews, of Kenyon College,
was the first citizen to offer his services to the State.

John Morgan, a dare-devil rebel general, with two thou-
and cavalry, made a raid through Southern Ohio in 1863,
estroying bridges and depots, cutting telegraph lines, burn-
ng factories and mills, and picking up the best horses. In
oing around Cincinnati, he traveled ninety miles in thirty-
ix hours. By these rapid and zigzag marches he eluded the
militia, until he attempted to recross the Ohio, near Parkers-
urg, where he was captured. He was imprisoned at Col-
mbus, but soon escaped.

Common Schools.

Although the first State constitution provided that
schools and the means of instruction shall forever be en-
ouraged by legislative provision," no bill for the establish-
nent of common schools was passed until 1825.

The State now assures to each pupil facilities for attend-
ng school six months each year.

51

The school year commences on the first day of September.

Legal holidays are Christmas, New Year's Day, May 30th, July 4th, February 22d, and Thanksgiving.

Township high schools may be established, and township superintendents employed.

The State is divided into the following school districts: city districts of the first class, city districts of the second class, village districts, special districts, and township districts. The township district is divided into sub-districts.

The salary of the State School Commissioner is $2,000, and $500 for traveling expenses. The term of the present Commissioner, Eli T. Tappan, commenced on the second Monday of July, 1887.

Ohio has three State colleges,—Ohio University, Miami University, and Ohio State University. Each had its origin in public land grants, and each has received legislative appropriations. Ohio University now has a Normal Department, established by the legislature in 1886. Ohio has more colleges than any other State.

School Funds.—The constitution provided that one section or the one thirty-sixth part of each township be devoted to the support of the public schools. The proceeds of the sale of these lands go to form a State irreducible fund, and each township gets six per cent. on its share. In case the lands remain unsold, the township gets the rent for the support of its schools.

Schools are supported by,

1. Interest on irreducible fund or rent.

2. A State tax of one mill on the dollar.

3. A contingent fund, not to exceed seven mills on the dollar, levied by boards of education.

4. Money derived from fines, licenses, and dog tax.

Educational Statistics, 1886.

School age, from 6 to 21 years.

School month, 4 weeks.

Youth of school age, 1,101,000.

Pupils enrolled, 775.000.

Average attendance, 518,000.

Teachers employed, 25,000.

Expenditures per year, $10,000,000.

Average weeks of school in State, 31.

Colored youth, 26,000.

School houses, 12,700.

Per cent. of attendance on enrollment, 67.

Per cent. of enrollment on enumeration, 71.

Average cost per capita on the average attendance, $17.

Per cent. of applications for certificates rejected, 45.

Smallest per cent., in Montgomery County, 14.

Largest per cent., in Scioto County, 67.

Colleges and Universities, 37.

Normal schools, 7.

Female institutions, 14.

Professional institutions, 18.

Educational Institutions, with Date of Founding.

Adelbert College, Wes'n Res. Univ.	Cleveland.	1826
Antioch College	Yellow Springs	1852
Baldwin University.	Berea.	1856
Belmont College	College Hill.	1846
Beverly College	Beverly	1842
Buchtel College	Akron	1870
Calvin College.	Brooklyn Village	1873
Capital University	Columbus	1850
Denison University	Granville	1831
Franklin College	New Athens.	1825
German Wallace College	Berea.	1864
Harlem Springs College	Harlem Springs	1858
Hebrew Union College	Cincinnati.	1873
Heidelberg College	Tiffin.	1850
Hiram College	Hiram	1867
Hopedale Normal College	Hopedale.	1852
Kenyon College	Gambier	1824
Marietta College.	Marietta	1835
Miami University.	Oxford	1809
Mount Union College.	Mount Union	1846
Muskingum College	New Concord.	1837
National Normal University	Lebanon	1855
Oberlin College.	Oberlin.	1833
Ohio State University.	Columbus	1870
Ohio University	Athens.	1804
Ohio Wesleyan University	Delaware.	1842
Otterbein University.	Westerville.	1847
Rio Grande College..	Rio Grande	1876
Saint Joseph College	Cincinnati	1873
Saint Xavier College.	Cincinnati	1831
Scio College.	Scio	1866
The University of Wooster	Wooster	1868
University of Cincinnati	Cincinnati	1870
Urbana University.	Urbana	1850
Wilberforce University.	Wilberforce	1856
Wilmington College	Wilmington.	1870
Wittenberg College	Springfield	1845
Findlay College	Findlay.	1886
Northeastern Ohio Normal School.	Canfield	1881
Ohio Normal University	Ada.	1871
Twin Valley College	Germantown	1886

54

Cincinnati Riot in 1884—Many citizens of Cincinnati were indignant because juries had failed to convict certain murderers. After a meeting in Music Hall on the evening of March 26, a mob went to the jail for the purpose of hanging a prisoner, but the man was secretly sent to Columbus. The mob tried to batter down the doors, and set the jail on fire. This was the beginning of a six days' riot in which the court-house was burned, forty-five people killed, and one hundred and thirty-eight wounded. The State militia was called out, but was, for a time, powerless.

Natural Gas.—The recent discovery of natural gas in many parts of the State may prove to be the beginning of a new era in manufacturing

Ohio River Floods.—In February, 1884, a general thaw and heavy rains caused the Ohio River to overflow its banks to an unusual extent. The destruction of property was great, and many lives were lost. Much of Cincinnati, including the gas works, was under water. At night the city was in darkness. The flood reached its climax on the 14th, when the river was seventy-one feet and three fourths of an inch above the low water mark.

Dow Law of 1886.—Local Option.—This law imposes a tax of two hundred dollars a year on saloons; makes it unlawful to sell liquor to minors, and empowers municipal corporations to prohibit the sale entirely within their corporate limits. Druggists may sell only on a physician's prescription or for mechanical purposes.

Facts About Ohio.—The "Buckeye State."—Latitude, 38° 26' to 41° 57' north.

Longitude, 80° 34' to 84° 49' west.

Greatest length from north to south, 225 miles.

Greatest breath from east to west, 200 miles.

Area, 41,060 square miles.

Average annual rain fall, 39 inches.

Average annual temperature, 51°.

Average elevation above the sea, 700 feet.

Highest point, in Logan County, 1,540 feet.

Lowest point, on the Ohio River, near Cincinnati, 433 feet.

Elevation of Lake Erie, 575 feet.

Rain-fall at Cincinnati, 44 inches.

Rain-fall at Lake Erie, 32 inches.

Number of United States representatives in Congress, 21.

Number of electoral votes, 23.

Square miles of coal measures, 11,000.

Number of counties, 88.

Population in 1800, 45,365.

Population in 1810, 230,760.

Population in 1880, 3,198,062.

The Ohio River extends along the southern border 436 miles.

Lake Erie has an Ohio shore line of 230 miles.

Population to square mile, 78.

Periodicals in 1886, 903.

Yearly death rate per 1,000 13.3.

Volunteers in Mexican War, 5,536.

Center of population of the United States, in 1880, eight miles west of Cincinnati.

The first law assessing a school tax was passed in 1825.

The first mail route through the interior was established over "Zane's trace" (226 miles) in 1799. Postage was from 6¼ to 25 cents, according to distance. Stamps were not in use. Under the old laws postage was not required to be paid in advance, but if it was prepaid the word "paid" was written on the outside of the letter by the postmaster. In ike manner the amount of postage was written on the corner of the letter.

Churches, 7,500.

Public charitable institutions, 317.

Value of taxable property (1885), $1,670,079,868.

Value of other property (1885), $78,000,000.

Rate of State tax, 2.9.

County taxes in 1885, $8,527,843.

City taxes, $7,771,601.

School taxes, $7,771,000.

Township taxes, $1,152,000; total taxes, $33,944,828.

Dogs taxed $1 each, 207,393.

Colored population in 1880, 80,000.   Indian, 130.

Legal interest rate, 6 per cent; by contract, 8 per cent.

Number of voters, 816,577.

Rank in agricultural implements and wool, 1.

In petroleum, iron, steel, wealth, and railroads, 2.

In wheat, sheep, coal, liquors, and population, 3.

In printing and publishing, salt, and soap, 4.

In milch cows, hogs, horses, hay, tobacco, and manufacturing, 5.

In area, 32; in age, 17.

Number of farms, 250,000.

Population of Cincinnati, the "Queen City of the West," 255,000.

Population of Cleveland, 160,000.

The Ohio Teachers' Association was organized at Akron, in 1847.

The first steamboat that navigated the Ohio River, the "Orleans," was built at Pittsburg, in 1811, and made her first trip to New Orleans in 1812.   It was several years later, however, before steamboats came into general use.

The first religious newspaper published in America was issued at Chillicothe, in 1814, and called *The Recorder*.

57

In 1834, the first steam-power printing press set up in the West was established at Cincinnati, for the publication of the *Gazette.*

Governors of Ohio.

1. Arthur St. Clair, Territorial........................1787—1802
2. Charles W. Byrd, Territorial........................1802—1803
3. Edward Tiffin, State........................1803—1807
4. Thomas Kirker, (acting)........................1807—1803
5. Samuel Huntington........................1808—1810
6. Return J. Meigs........................1810—1814
7. O. Looker, (acting)........................1814—
8. Thomas Worthington........................1814—1818
9. Ethan Allen Brown........................1818—1822
10. Allen Trimble, (acting)........................1822—
11. Jeremiah Morrow........................1822—1826
12. Allen Trimble........................1826—1830
13. Duncan McArthur........................1830—1832
14. Robert Lucas........................1832—1836
15. Joseph Vance........................1836—1838
16. Wilson Shannon........................1838—1840
17. Thomas Corwin........................1840—1842
18. Wilson Shannon........................1842—1844
19. Thomas W. Bartley, (acting)........................1844—
20. Mordecai Bartley........................1844—1846
21. William Webb........................1846—1849
22. Seabury Ford........................1849—1850
23. Reuben Wood........................1850—1853
24. William Medill........................1853—1856
25. Salmon P. Chase........................1856—1860
26. William Dennison........................1860—1862
27. David Tod........................1862—1864
28. John Brough........................1864—1865
29. Charles Anderson, (acting)........................1865—1866
30. J. D. Cox........................1866—1868
31. R. B. Hayes........................1868—1872
32. Edward F. Noyes........................1872—1874
33. William Allen........................1874—1876
34. R. B. Hayes........................1876—1878
35. R. M. Bishop........................1878—1880
36. Charles Foster........................1880—1884
37. George Hoadly........................1884—1886
38. J. B. Foraker........................1886—

Counties and County Seats.

County	Seat	County	Seat
Adams	West Union.	Licking	Newark.
Allen	Lima.	Logan	Bellefontaine.
Ashland	Ashland.	Lorain	Elyria.
Ashtabula	Jefferson.	Lucas	Toledo.
Athens	Athens.	Madison	London.
Auglaize	Wapakoneta.	Mahoning	Youngstown.
Belmont	St. Clairsville.	Marion	Marion.
Brown	Georgetown.	Medina	Medina.
Butler	Hamilton.	Meigs	Pomeroy.
Carroll	Carrollton.	Mercer	Celina.
Champaign	Urbana.	Miami	Troy.
Clarke	Springfield.	Monroe	Woodsfield.
Clermont	Batavia.	Montgomery	Dayton.
Clinton	Wilmington.	Morgan	McConnellsville.
Columbiana	New Lisbon.	Morrow	Mt. Gilead.
Coshocton	Coshocton.	Muskingum	Zanesville.
Crawford	Bucyrus.	Noble	Caldwell.
Cuyahoga	Cleveland.	Ottawa	Port Clinton.
Darke	Greenville.	Paulding	Paulding.
Defiance	Defiance.	Perry	New Lexington.
Delaware	Delaware.	Pickaway	Circleville.
Erie	Sandusky.	Pike	Waverly.
Fairfield	Lancaster.	Portage	Ravenna.
Fayette	Washington C. H.	Preble	Eaton.
Franklin	Columbus.	Putnam	Ottawa.
Fulton	Wauseon.	Richland	Mansfield.
Gallia	Gallipolis.	Ross	Chillicothe.
Geauga	Chardon.	Sandusky	Fremont.
Greene	Xenia.	Scioto	Portsmouth.
Guernsey	Cambridge.	Seneca	Tiffin.
Hamilton	Cincinnati.	Shelby	Sidney.
Hancock	Findlay.	Stark	Canton.
Hardin	Kenton.	Summit	Akron.
Harrison	Cadiz.	Trumbull	Warren.
Henry	Napoleon.	Tuscarawas	New Philadelphia.
Highland	Hillsboro.	Union	Marysville.
Hocking	Logan.	Van Wert	Van Wert.
Holmes	Millersburg.	Vinton	McArthur.
Huron	Norwalk.	Warren	Lebanon.
Jackson	Jackson.	Washington	Marietta.
Jefferson	Steubenville.	Wayne	Wooster.
Knox	Mt. Vernon.	Williams	Bryan.
Lake	Painesville.	Wood	Bowling Green.
Lawrence	Ironton.	Wyandot	Upper Sanudsky.